A Special Friend

Les Howard

Illustrated by David House

Dominie Press, Inc.

The development of the *Carousel Readers* was supported by the Reading Recovery project at California State University, San Bernardino. All authors' royalties from the sale of the *Carousel Readers* will be used to support various Reading Recovery projects.

Publisher: Raymond Yuen
Illustrator: David House
Cover Designer: Pamela Pettigrew-Norquist

Copyright © 1995 Dominie Press, Inc.

All rights reserved. No part of this publication may be reproduced or transmitted in any form or by any means without permission in writing from the publisher. Reproduction of any part of this book, through photocopy, recording, or any electronic or mechanical retrieval system, without the written permission of the publisher is an infringement of the copyright law.

Published by

Dominie Press, Inc.
5945 Pacific Center Boulevard
San Diego, California 92121 USA

ISBN 1-56270-374-9
Printed in Singapore by PH Productions.

1 2 3 4 5 6 7 PH 98 97 96 95

I have a friend,
a very special friend.
She is black and white
and has a loud bark.

When she was a puppy,
she was so small
I could put her in my pocket.

Now she is big.
She chases balls
and digs holes.

She has a basket to sleep in, but I always let her sleep on my bed.

She is always happy to see me when I get home from school. Everyone loves my dog.

Even my cat.